the slow knot of time

Poems by Martin Jones

Cyberwit.net
HIG 45 Kaushambi Kunj, Kalindipuram
Allahabad - 211011 (U.P.) India
http://www.cyberwit.net
Tel: +(91) 9415091004
E-mail: info@cyberwit.net

Printed in India at Vcore Connect LLP.

To Pamela

Contents

False Spring Day in February 7

Lost City 8

Congo 10

Rest With Me, Love 12

If I Could 13

The Devil Enters Time 14

Star Travelers 16

The Coconuts Are Singing 17

In the Hamburg Train Station 21

Cadillac Dreaming 22

Backwards Into Fate 24

Whistling Over Scrub 27

Searching for Camus 29

An Aging House Cat Reflects 30

Asphalt Dreams 32

A Squat Man, A Whiskey Drinker 35

Existing 37

Dancing Eyes 39

Young Man on a Road Crew 40

Covid Summer 42

Notes Of A Distant Country 44

Still Life in Lockdown 46

The Rooming Houses of Our Early Years 48

The Road from Toronto to Ottawa 50

Seafarers 52

Darkness Visible 53

My Cynical Friend the Sex Tourist 54

Sailing on the Danforth 56

The Smile 57

What Lies Between 58
The Way of All Guys 60

Poems For Younger Folk

I've Been to the Attic 64
Red-Winged Blackbird 65
I wish … 66
My Happy Birdfeeder 67
Visit to the Mall. 68
The Stars in Summer 69
Leaping Love 70
Geese in the Night 71
Posted During Covid 19 72
A Path in the Woods 73
Autumn in the City 74

False Spring Day in February

I've walked this path before
in angular sun and soft, watery
haze, but cannot remember when.
The smell of earth mixes with the
melting snow and the brave
enduring scent of rock and brook.

I step carefully by the bits of icy slick
that cling to leaves and mud-strewn trail.
I try but cannot trick myself today;
it is only a winter's afternoon.
The chill settles early on the chest
and preternatural shadows race
along a nearby ridge.

My thoughts should be homeward, yet
the silence holds me in its hush, the
only sounds the muffled gurgle
of the creek and unheard songs of
April finch and summer wren;

And in the not-quite dusk that falls
about the brooding trees, there is a
moment's glimpse of what, I cannot
say, but lies beyond the languid
blue slow knot of time or maybe not,
before the presage of nightfall's
wind-blown drifts settling in again.

Lost City

Sometimes I come upon it without thinking,
glancing down an alleyway or passing
a forgotten railway spur as light slants toward
afternoon. More often, it will be turning
a corner and seeing what isn't there, say, a
slapped-up blue stand, groaning with a
hundred-weight of wide-papered broadsheets
and magazines long dead; and then the
broken, jagged shouts of the hawker with
his stubble and his wet cigar.

It was a small, mean city, I suppose, the
Toronto of my childhood, worn and shabby
before the soaring steel towers, the glass
and the fine-grained presumptions;
a decaying mouth of broken molars or a
gambler's toss of stubby office blocks and
greasy spoons, fading, drab hotels with
drowsy coffee shops and in the lobby waiting
patiently, a sad-faced card shark in double
checks and two-toned shoes.

Yet, an honest city for all that, a city that
beyond its core smoked and belched and
roared, a city of lathes and forges that ground
out such things a good-hearted working man
might afford. An honest harbour too, echoing
with the shouts of longshoreman and sailors from

the ore boats and brewing with the sweet
brown refining stench of sugar and malt.

I did not love it then, but love it now. I see it
as it was, a beast grappling for a handhold, a
city bellowing the cry of a vanishing age.

Congo

The road winds north through rain forest
and like a highway, is numbered
though barely wide enough to contain twin ruts for truck wheels.
We are a month into the dry season
yet the way is blocked in many places
by deep pools of mud and toppled branches
and everywhere one looks is jungle:
shimmering, green-roiled and pregnant, impenetrable.

Our two Landcruisers have been left with the drivers
so we will walk the last hour of our journey.
Once underway, you wish never to cease walking
for the morning is unusually soft and translucent,
cool, and the air intoxicates.

We pass three villages sheltered in forest clearings near the road,
each a smattering of tiny homes of mud and wattle.
These are shy folk who live so far from anywhere,
they look away at first, then smile, grow warm and welcoming;
the children approach us slowly and giggle.

Further on, the roadway dips toward a valley
shaded in forest canopy and silence.
It is then we see them, three in the lead,
tall, willowy, furious men moving quickly toward us on foot,
and then more, a dozen appearing around a bend,
followed by a gaggle of long-horned, skinny, rib-jutting cattle
who trot hurriedly behind.

These men are clothed in yellowing brown rags
that barely hang together
yet they tower over us as they pass.
Everything about this is startling, an apparition out of time.
We know who they are, Tutsi cattle herders from Rwanda,
wandering outcasts
in relentless search of grazing land.
All who are with me are Congolese and they have heard only stories;
never before have they encountered such men.

There is no way of knowing whether this resolute band
arrived in Congo the week before last, or like ghosts,
have been wandering these primeval ways
generation to generation,
since before even the Belgians arrived.

They bestow not a moment's glance on us
but rush past in furious ensemble,
a curdled loathing on curled mouths,
enraged with what, we are not sure
though the contempt is strangely wounding.
Possibly, they do not regard us as human and consider
it profane to pollute their eyes with our presence.
Or perhaps they fear us, for hatreds simmer unspoken
in this brooding and brutal land
where it once was not unknown, I've been told,
for some to slit a Tutsi herder's throat without a thought
and who knows when such men may come again.

Rest With Me, Love

Rest with me, love, gently by my side;
let loose your silking hair and lay your
head weary on my willing shoulder.
The sun has paced its fervid rounds
and morning stands far-off as eternity.
In this moment, lit-softly and self-
contained, time forfeits all measure
and heartbreak its sting. All nature rests,
as I rest with you, love, in this silence
that bears neither writ nor summons,
belonging to you and to me alone.

If I Could

If I l could I would stark,
enduring words of
love sail forth in towered
galleons to breach
the ocean lying between,
verse and song of
tempered hues as only
you and the wind
might comprehend

And listening far off
you might fancy that
once I loved you or given
half a chance should love
you in some time to come,
or you might surmise
my love is out of time and
sings in this solitary moment
concealing timelessness.

If I could.

The Devil Enters Time

We were fishing off dânus brçhwâ, too humble
to call a bridge, casting for perch and pickerel
and talking such nonsense as boys talk, of
county fairs and wild horses, of whom among
gods is fiercest and among girls the loveliest,
a morning made for fishing, no rain for days, no
clouds, just a wayward breeze and the sun.

Who was first to fall silent? Was it the crow or
the morning dove, the village dogs or perhaps
the cicadas by the road? Maybe it was us.
Later, we said our shivering was from the cold
but we knew it was fear; even the sun hid itself
in a sudden cloud as the ominous slow click-clog
began, soft at first, growing towards scrapes and
moans; all nature heard it with us, a being
trudging slowly in pain, dragging a foot behind,
flinging its twisted body forward in slow-motion.
At bridge-top the head swiveled toward us with
a leer of broken teeth; there were no eyes but
pools of death and lamentation without end.
I vomited when it was gone, you shivered once
more and slowly, the morning re-assembled itself.

Yet I wonder if it was really you and I on that
bridge so many summers ago, for it seems a time
beyond recollection. The story has been told in
so many places and for so long, by my grandfather
and his grandfather, one imagines it to be a tale

from the far edge of memory that in a lost clearing
along the Nile valley or in Ur's primordial Eden,
two boys were fishing off a bridge when the devil
passed by, foreseeing this singular event
to be sufficient.

Star Travelers

We are star-travellers,
brief-lived, unknowing,
come hurtling through brute
time and boundless void,
riding an obscure star
that has since time began
coursed the reaches of 100
billion stars in all, sailing the
far frontier of a galaxy
woven from the celestial trance
of giant sun-wheels spinning
an eternal dance.

Our guide and consolation is
a transient grace, insisting
that all exists for *Now*,
for this momentary bliss,
for those whom we adore
and perhaps a backwards kiss,
a transitory passing
like the slanting light at dusk
and then it's gone and on and on,
times without number more
this simple star must
revolve before star-spinning
slowly spirals into dust.

[Our Sun and solar system orbits around the center of the Milky
Way galaxy at an average velocity of 828,000 km/hr, taking about
230 million years to make one complete orbit. The Milky Way is a
spiral galaxy of 100 billion stars.]

The Coconuts Are Singing

I was so aimless
as a kid, so aimless, driftless,
lazy and shiftless
that I merited such warnings
from fathers, uncles, teachers,
principals and perfect strangers as
they saw fit to deliver,
grimacing in my direction,
then gazing reflectively
out a window and
announcing, "You know, son,
it's awfully cold digging ditches
this time of year."
But I was not worried, for
ditches were an artifact
of the past.

Still, there was a fear,
secret, anguished and terrifying,
that shook me awake
at three in the mornings;
a vision of a future where I was
condemned to wander
from door-to-suburban-door
hawking Fuller brushes,
marching daily through
a forgotten circle of Dante's hell
fashioned for shy and
distracted introverts like myself

who found themselves
wanting at whatever talents
were required for worldly
endeavours. Such thoughts
tortured me daily,
and not just to the bone,
but to the very marrow.

Thus, I turned 20, too gloomy
to celebrate with anything like
the spinning joy of later
birthdays but instead was staying
with an uncle, searching for
work and what do you know?
Like an Ophidiophobiac
drawn to the snake house in a zoo,
I answered an ad to become
a Fuller brush salesman.

In eight hours of hesitant
and stuttering salesmanship,
I sold not a single brush
nor even a solitary bristle,
but watched in wonder as
Murray my mentor succeeded
in unloading suitcases full of
hair-brushes, scrub-brushes,
toilet brushes and potato-peelers,
cajoling, cadoodalling and teasing
lovely young housewives
out of their sugar bowl savings.

How I marvelled at Murray,
wiry-whippet and red coiffed,
as he danced from house to house,
exuberant and joyful, a blowfish
puffed and propelled beyond
reason, a man who knew his
calling and adored it.

Not so myself, and thus was I
amazed when Murray
invited me to his apartment
for a beer. Even more amazing
was the photograph of a
gorgeous wife in her nurse's cap,
sitting on the sideboard,
and her tender love letter
waiting on the dining room table,
which Murray proceeded
to read to me, not once
but thrice, and what
a revelation. This paragon
of beauty, this Nightingale,
wrote like the very
incarnation of Shakespeare.
"How is this possible that Murray
should have such a wondrous
wife?" I asked my uncle. "How?"
"The world's a stage, old son,"
laughed my uncle from beneath
wry and furry Glaswegian eyebrows,
"full of miracles and make-believe
and today you were given
a seat in the very first row,"

all of which made me think
that this business of
making a living might
be far more entertaining than
I had appreciated and what's
more, I had for eight hours
stared into the abyss and
walked away whole.

Now this was a long time ago
indeed. As for Murray,
I remember him fondly and often
think of him as I threaten
my own son that if he does not
hoist his socks he will one
day fritter away his life as
a Fuller brush man, though
I suspect he has no idea
what that is. And as I hear
myself yammering forth, I
remember Murray shouting
lustily whenever we passed a
variety store, "Look at that
lost soul, all day long he waits
for customers to come to him,
but we head straight to their
front doors that's how damn
smart we are. A world of coconuts
awaits the plucking, my young
friend – a world of coconuts, listen
and you can hear them
singing your name."

In the Hamburg Train Station

Not yet 6 am and two laughing, ribald lads in black tie
and tuxedos come bounding into the Hamburg train
station delirious with fraternal love for all, declaiming
joyously to me and then to the old man walking behind,
though far more grandly in his case as the proclamation
descends from the summit of a gargantuan leap, W*ir
sind betrunken, Opa* and despite the old fellow waving
them away like sand flies, exultant they remain, for it is
a fact that drunkenness and its raptures have been discovered
by humans this very morning and though the fearsome,
exuberant pair are being taken by respectable Hamburg
commuters as insufferable louts, I am younger even than
these lads and would prefer nothing better than to go
blissfully leaping after them toward whatever tavern
and sweet-faced young Frauleins might await at this
undrinkable hour of morning but am fortunately
restrained by *mein Deutsch* which is fit for only slow and
sober contemplation, but will soon, I have been assured,
find the words for youthful things that need no words,
exultation and glorious abandon being chief among them.

Cadillac Dreaming

On the morning of my daughter's
birth my father touched down in
a Cadillac – sky-blue and
sleek-finned, irreductable, molecular
in essence and
announced it had forever
been his dream to pilot
such a celestial beast
on the occasions of his
elevation to grand-fatherdom.
No one believed this
beatific vision, least of all
my mother, but looking back now
I see the inspiration of
Cadillacs in the creamy Impalas
and bottle-blue Buicks, in the balloon-
red Parisiennes
that had been my father's
to acquire and sell year after
year, remembering in particular a panel
on a '57 Chevy so turquoise you
could swim through it to the sky.

My father's Cadillac was a great star-
going galleon of pistons and silence;
he was the skipper; famous
down the Florida coast,
cruising over continents, and
hovering over days of toil

until finally he grew too old
for Cadillac dreaming
and auctioned the hulk for
two hundred dollars, saying that's
an end to it. And so it was
for three weeks
when he emerged from the doors of
Cadillac II whose sheen and dimensions
were even more transcendent
than the first – a divine
transport of sensors and gauges.
From the summit of microchip Olympus
he computed his most recent
parsec per gallon. Then with seatbelts
secured, the old man flicked the antigravity.
The sparks flew like a parting benediction
and away he soared
to the shooting blue firmament.

Backwards Into Fate

I used to imagine him
strolling into bistros and cafes,
being warmly greeted
by fellow diners,
(a tonic to those who
work alone).
It was always summer
in these thoughts
and I recall that he favored
silk Hawaiian shirts, wore them
year-round in fact.
He believed that it was
how one lived that counted,
and not the fame,
thus, he traveled much, for
adventure and for inspiration.
Summers in Cape Breton,
(his cabin looked east
toward Port Hood)
and every January third
departing for the south of Spain.
A small flat had been
retained in the city
not far from where
we sit right now,
to visit old friends,
for the galleries and concerts
and taking care of business.
For there was much business,

you'd be surprised by
all the irons in the fire.
Once, by a window in a coffee shop
I thought I might linger and
surprise him as he passed,
an impossibility I know.

Odd how we always picture
such folk alone in their
perfect, clairvoyant lives,
often making ready to leave,
stepping from a front porch
toward days of
impossible merit
or waving exuberantly
from the bow of a ship
about to sail. Still, so alike
were we it's strange
the fellow never took a wife
as beautiful as mine or
fathered children, who,
considering the years
now gone would be grown
with families of their own.
It never occurred that it
might be his that was
the pallid, insipid life,
favoring freedom merely
in the way some men
like their whiskey served.

As for most, it seems we
are forever starting over,

hoping to get it right this time,
until starting over
becomes our lives.
Thus, slowly we stumble
toward understanding,
for there is much
to be said in praise
of these lives we come by,
these blind, donkey lives
with their fiascos
and their sting.
Our joys are more
finely-tempered for being
fewer and hard-earned
and conceal a singular,
compelling music
of their own, like the
unexpected glimpse
of those we love,
caught unawares and
lost in laughter.
*Marching Backwards
Into Fate* – a fine operating
manual for any age.

Whistling Over Scrub

(A Homage to Robert Frost)

On a somnolent summer's afternoon
without a care to blot the sun,
the red-winged blackbirds flashing
low and whistling over scrub,
I dawdled on a country road
as rumbling freight clanked dumbly
past, so many cars there were
I could not count them all
but saw them born from billowed
skies far off and for a moment
fancied that their hulls
were bulging with the dreams of
everyone I'd ever loved.
I wondered where the rail-line
led but sadly knew
it was merely through the summer
haze beyond to an abandoned
siderail by a toppled shed.

That's enough of dreaming, I told
myself, I've over-gorged on my fair
share plus more, yet dreaming is
a habit we cannot shake or maybe
it is dreams that cannot shake we
humans off.

That's a thought – that stuff
as dreams exist like notes and numbers

in Platonic form and would just as
soon we bugger off. So here I am,
so many years and more, persisting
once again to dream such odds and
ends as rarely rhyme yet what else
but that and love will carry us aloft
above Chronos and his unremitting crime.

Searching for Camus

I passed by Algiers only once, 19
years old and unaware you had ever
lived, knew nothing of Sisyphus or
the absurd or of thoughts as crystalline
as glacier water. A white-washed
city rising from the sea, Ikósion
to the Greeks, but first it was
Phoenician and later Roman,
Ottoman, French, Algerian.
I wandered up and down the
medina's steep and winding ways,
by the Grand Mosque and
Catholic basilica and along the
sun-steeped harbour.

I go searching for you sometimes,
my friend, wandering these ways
again, through the park and past
the old train station, along the seashore,
then cityward. I saw you only once,
not on the football pitch as I'd hoped,
leaping for the ball, intent, liberated,
your labyrinthic thoughts left behind.
It was at the aérodrome. You stood
aloof, looking away, a man under
suspicion, waiting for the Paris flight.

An Aging House Cat Reflects

Dug into darkness, blanket-swathed
and curled within this warm
sleeping being whose affections are felt
deep within I am
hypnotic with dreams
of floating yellow-streaked moons
that sing me forth,
of nights crazy-ripe, explosive
in the noble smells of soil and wild grass,
in the sweet beckoning scent of wind.
I am delirious with long-ago memory,
of chasing darting long-tailed creatures
and of beings who love and touch and smell
as I and that I shall never see again.

In dark mulling spaces I take refuge
where longings wander in what
I wonder ... the where-ness?
At times I dash ... this way and that.

I draw smells and meaty brown textures
into me, full-bellied, satiated,
sitting with the looming, indifferent
being, the one who rules,
hand upon my spine, stroking.

Sounds call ... darkness draws me toward itself.
Loud noises, sudden and smashing, terrify.
All extends outwards
from this wondering-place,

from the not-right sense
that I belong not here but elsewhere
under some wilder, witching sky.

Asphalt Dreams

By the Otonabee and Trent I lingered six months, scrabbling
together paychecks and daydreams, thinking of the curving
road that waited by the city limits, marking the night hours
in a blue stucco rooming house. At the edge of town was an
old asbestos factory where one could find work, a steaming,
creaking Victorian affair grinding out brake shoes for trucks and
locomotives and when the asbestos rose in clouds a man would
sweat like a ripe hog in his mask.

We admired the older workers for they carried themselves
with dignity and no longer sought illusion or pretense. I remember
Gordy, an Ojibwe farmer who wore a tattoo on his forearm
with the names of his army buddies in Korea; I asked about it
once; I did not dare ask again.

In those years, one touched each day silently, like a bead on a
necklace, and thus, slowly, time fell away. March arrived and
in the evenings you stepped outside and smelled in the spring air
the gravel and tar of the highway. I would read until ten, walk
out for a beer with friends. So damned happy were we then,
imagining we'd live forever. There was an old bar we favored,
The New Grand Hotel, but I'm told it's long gone.

Truck drivers tell the best stories, honest, good-hearted tales,
it must be all that solitude makes them loquacious. A gruff-as-hell
Teamster based out of LaSalle, en route to Sudbury, relayed to
me his life, pretty much start to finish.

*The old man back in Cornerbrook pleaded with me to take up
the family business, learn the ropes, but I was too clever for my
own good – had the idea of heading for the Big Smoke and making
it rich. It was some fun back then, believe it old son, the bars, the
buddies I made and all the sweet girls I knew, some good
Newfoundlanders living there, 'til it wasn't. Every few months I
haul into Toronto. Keep planning to look up the old crew.
Maybe next time.*

High along the Queen Elizabeth range near Jaspar on a bicycle
I met some oil workers on a holiday, two Nigerians and a youth
from Kashmir. All of us young, starting out. It was early morning
and near the top of a mountain we paused for a few seconds
on our bikes, thick mist and cloud below, readying ourselves,
about to swoop in a rush downwards like gulls or maybe more
like angels for rarely are we given the gift of knowing the magical
or the transcendent or the spiritual or whatever you want to call it,
or maybe it's simply the exultation of existing for a pure,
celestial moment without limits.

It was a bleak rain in Winnipeg and I found the last space on the
floor of a hostel for the night. There were two lads living rough,
one much bigger than the other and owning nothing more than a
change of socks and the shoes on their feet. One of them had come by
an old Gideon's bible and asked about the passage where the lord
is my shepherd, I shall not want. I read it slowly through, out loud.
The small lad said: *I remember those words from the foster homes.*
The big fellow asked me to recite it again. *Surely goodness and mercy
shall follow me all the days of my life*, I read as he glanced into space.

Somewhere south of Wawa and north of the Soo and just before
sunset I hitched a ride with a hard rock miner and his girl friend.
He was mid-aged, tall and red-faced, spoke with a Geordie accent;

she was much younger than him and for a time afterwards I'd dream of her dark Chilean eyes and quick smile. For a long while on the road we laughed big whooping car-rocking guffaws at his stories from the north of England and of the copper and nickel mines of Ontario, tales that were not merely tall, but rose higher than the CN Tower.

Let me tell you, he began one improbable yarn *of the time I was lifted royally up a mine shaft on an easy-chair in honour of my poker prowess.*

But my new friends were only going so far and soon I was roadside again, thumb stuck out in the dark, waiting for a ride. But who's going to trust a stranger on a road lit only by the moon and stars? I began to walk and kept it up for hours and was happy for the solitude. I recall how a trace of the sun never left the mid-summer sky that night, even in the smallest hours of the morning. The dawn came early, around four am, spreading its reddish-amber glow through the clouds and across the eastern horizon.

It stayed like that for a long, long while before the sun finally rose in the hills.

A Squat Man, A Whiskey Drinker

He's a squat man, broad across the chest, grizzled,
a whiskey drinker I notice from the empty bottles
lying near our feet; he tells me he rolls his own,
Player's Fine, what else? He coughs and waves
a short, stubby hand across a sweep of barren
farmland. *Everything I own is in this venture,* he says
Where you see weeds, son, I see the future.

He's right about the weeds — I see little here but
pigweed and pokeweed, sorrel and thistle stretching
far across farmland toward distant pine trees.
Gravel too, a pile of old tires and a rusted-out
silver trailer, into which he invites me, being both
his office and his domicile.

They'll be an airport here one day, he announces
as he fires up a burner to heat a chipped-blue
coffee pot with yellow flower decals on the side.
*You just wait and see. Not a two-bit airstrip
for Sunday pilots with their Piper cubs. No sir.
A real airport. Great flying cargo ships and passenger
jets lining up to refuel on their way over North America.*

Coffee cups in hand, we study the yellowing map lying
on the drafting desk. He points to the airport in Gander,
Newfoundland and then to Texas and Minneapolis
and says *Look, half-way between.* Next, he unfurls
the ancient blueprints. A rectangle represents
the passenger lounge and offices; a circle stands for

the control tower and the large narrow oval, shaped
like a lemon lozenge, is the runway. An arrow
points the way south to the St Lawrence River.

*Can you write a bang-up article, son, one that
wakes up those arrogant bastards in Ottawa?
Let them know we need this airport. Best publish
it on the front page.* I tell him I'll do my best and
he accompanies me to the car, pausing briefly
to admire his kingdom of scrub. *Damn it, this is my
dream, son, and you can't stop a man from dreaming.*
"No, sir, you can't," I say. *Good luck then.* He smiles
as he closes the driver's door for me.

It's thirty minutes to the newspaper office and
I drive more slowly than intuition advises,
this being only the second day of my first job.
The road winds past tidy farmland; and
the occasional stand of pine and hardwood trees
softens the landscape and gives it contour.
I am thinking of what I'll write, of how he seems
to be a good-hearted sort and I don't wish
to portray him as a fool, though it is late in the day
and no Trans-Atlantic flight needs refueling in
Gander nor here either in eastern Ontario.

I'm aware this assignment is a test or perhaps a practical
joke, a way of putting one over on the new guy.
I know too that no matter what I write,
if I write anything, the article will die in the trash can,
just as I'm certain this tale of a crazy, old man who
dreams of big silver jets descending from the sky
has died there times before.

Existing ...

It's hard to explain to those folks who just
aren't, those fanciful beings
of an illusory sort,
try and explain what it's like to just 'be,'
for it's all such an oddness,
even though it comes free.

It's a little like being your own house,
for everything's there, tasting and
feeling and looking all round;
there's touching and smells
and best of all sounds
like music and laughter
of affable friends
who drop in to visit
and never wear frowns.

But that's only part of it,
for there are also those
who wish they'd never
been born, for existing can
pierce your wits like a thorn,
indifferent, plug-empty,
too heavy, in pain;
it can cause quite a snit
if your life doesn't fit.

But there's much more, so please
comprehend, if you find yourself

puzzled by what it means in the end,
for there's caresses and passion,
and grievous grief over loss,
the solace of sun on our faces
till "chop" comes the toss.

But I still haven't nailed it quite
as I'd like, for there's wondering
too if we've got it just right,
for what if we too
are just fanciful beings
conjured up for a moment's refrain
out of some giant's celestial brain,
just dreams within dreams
without ever an end,
till existing goes puff
as giant wakes with a scream.

Dancing Eyes

Once were oceans where we lie,
plesiosaurs darted blindly by;
you can see them if you try.

Once were mountains fierce as dread
above this dale that holds our bed,
wild places where the mammoths fed.

Once were glaciers towering high
now floats the moon on star-mad skies,
this simple room, your dancing eyes

Young Man on a Road Crew

We were tailor-made to provoke his fury
I suppose, yet how could we from outside
his tiny world know? My wife and I
in a frivolous, fanciful mood on a sunny August
morning in Maine, the Damariscotta River and
a family visit behind us, a short drive and
and afternoon flight ahead.

I saw the young man fifty feet away, a road
worker who had dropped whatever task he
did to sneer in our direction. I feared he
might leap toward us zombie-like and as we
passed so slowly by, his face screwed
strangely flush with rage, I had to stare, and
then the scream: "Old dead Jew."

Later, we wondered if perhaps my white
beard and glasses were too scholarly for
the chap. Did the Massachusetts plate
on our rental car offend? Or maybe the fact
the sub-compact we planned to rent was not
available and so we happily piloted
a Lincoln SUV in bold maroon.

The rage perhaps I understand, a wealthy
old couple, to him at least, passes by, smug,
from out-of-state and flaunting an imaginary life
he will never see, old rich farts in a luxury car,
useless as sin, their good fortune no doubt

undeserved, and probably sneering at his
humble lot.

But that other thing, that rank and ancient
smear? I have tried to think it through but
am left bewildered with this single thought:
that to this young man, Jews are no more
than words on websites, imaginary beings to
rake and roil his hate, unaware he is merely
a pawn in play along with thousands and
millions more like him, knowing nothing
of the past, unable to distinguish truth from lies,
ignorant of Jewish legacy and faith, unaware
 of what gross sufferings are being
stoked with the likes of his pathetic mob.

My wife asks: where are we going, not expecting
an answer, least of all 'Toronto'. Down which
ugly road does the world now wind? And
toward what end? In Cairo, in Cologne,
in Moscow and Montreal and on and on,
foul and grasping men stir the pot, tending
the hateful brew that boils toward the brim.
The road worker I understand, though
not quite forgive, a fool and fodder for those
who scheme and smack their lips, the beasts
who pace the abattoirs of history, watching
sharp-eyed and waiting to be summoned,
finally, fully, from the dead.

Covid Summer

words so easily bewitch a chap
a normal lad like you or me
consider that I ambled
amiably the wrong way down
the grocery aisle on a
summer's afternoon, no harm
intended when a tiny sour-faced
old soul roiling in road-rage
took umbrage, screeching
"follow the arrows, moron,"
and raising her umbrella
épée-like barked, "prêt"
as she lunged menacingly
forward whereas I, no slow
dolt but quick as a bolt
from a crossbow, latched
for my defence upon a flys-
watter that was hanging
in a display wondering
flyswatter, *flyce water?*
what does water have to do
with flies as she bunged me
corps-a-corps with a stab to the
solar plexus and dashed off
screaming "help help help
there's a violet man in aisle 4,"
whereupon I, lying ventriculus
and ventricumbent,
wondered if she did not perhaps

mean violent or maybe verminous
or vituperative or vapid
vainglorious villainous vexatious
vicious or verbonious
and then quite naturally I enquired
of the clerk as he was about to
vault me thither have you ever
considered, sir, how many
scurrilous words begin with
the letter "v" but he
proved a rather deaf fellow and
told me that nothing is free,
not even the flyswatter I was
clutching to my side and
as I repatriated it forthwith
he wondered aloud how it
had come by its strange and
melodious name, *"flyce water,"*
he said, "what have flies to do
with water?" adding slowly,
"flyce, splice, mice, spice, dice,"
and what could we do next
but roll heavenward this curious
epiphany of nothing at all in a
Gregorian chant of appreciation.

Notes Of A Distant Country

The presentation is over and the lights flick on,
though my title slide still illuminates the screen,
The Country Where I Come From.
The talk has been a fizzle of maps and statistics, life
expectancies, annual incomes, crops grown and
oil imported. Tomorrow, no one will remember a thing.

Still, I am heartened by the lively curiosity of these
students; these are the lucky ones, impatiently
awaiting the end of childhood, wandering
restlessly about their labyrinthic dreams.

I ask for questions and they begin in familiar ways,
as do my answers, which follow with a recital of the
famous and infamous of a strange and distant country,
wars fought and battles won; our wonderous bicameral
legislature receives its plaudits, as do my comments
on the careers that await our gifted youth.

But the tall young man at the back of the room
is having none of it. For several minutes he has been
waving his arm about, anxious for my attention.
"And what of laughing and dancing and forgetting?"
he asks.

A moment's pause and a young woman speaks.
"Tell us about music in your country, how songs whisper
your fate from the darkest of dark places, from hidden
groves and alleyways, and does tomorrow promise to be
more perfect than all the days that have never been?"

"And what of the snow in winter," asks another.
Does it fall gently toward the end of day
and rest on the branches of Spruce and hardwood trees?
And does the slant of February light give snow
the slightest tint of blue as dusk approaches,
so that one becomes oddly melancholy and
longs for Spring?"

All hands are up and there are more questions
than I can parry. What of the luminescence of
glaciers and does the moon float on a cobalt
sky and does love really go on after we are dead?
So many questions and I do my best to reply,
though it seems my answers are falling short.

"And where do we begin and how will we know?"
They ask. "What is the route and what must we pack?"
All this and more, I assure them. There is an X in the fold
in the crease in the corner in the valley on a map and
it is never what you imagine. Wait, and slowly,
at its own pace, the journey makes itself known.

Still Life in Lockdown

I wonder what a drone might think sitting
on the wall, a tiny sort of chap,
fashioned like a greasy, common fly,
and steered by shifts of keening spies
buried deep within the FBI.

They'd guess our lives just bob along –
a blur of plodding projects where all
and nothing counts, for there's no lack
of things to read on mobile phones,
or drawing pictures, writing poems,
fresh games of chess wait for us to play
against computers worlds away,
John King at noon with all the stats,
(we love that magic wall of maps),
a nap, a chore, a phone call to the family doc
can gobble hours off the clock,
then 6 pm – man, cocktail hour truly rocks!

Dinner at seven and dishes at eight,
a Zoom with friends if it's not too late;
there's lightening tonight –
we count the seconds before the thunder;
we'll be lost in projects
'til we're shovelled under.

It's here the poor FBI spy looks away,
turns ashen-faced speaking with a friend,
"Foolish folks, there's nothing there

but empty gestures filling air,"
then adds only half in jest:
"So, don't mind me if I step onto the stairs
and blow out my brains in bleak despair."

(Though one day he may come to comprehend
that bricks and plaster hem you in
but imagination dashes toward the stars
and unlike Covid has no end.)

The Rooming Houses of Our Early Years

At times I remember the sequence of rooms where
we waited for life to finally resume, lying on a bed
in a space, no longer a youth and not quite a man,
gazing at clouds through a slit in the blinds,
motionless dust, a rattling fan.

Sundays were a slow turning of sun, of glare un-
remitting, though we sought not to grouse, for many
souls stumble through archipelagos of house
after house, a trial out-lasting all sense and reason,
persisting through the driest of seasons.

In one place a quiet man ate only ice cream, we talked
of nutrition *aber nicht verstehen, no listen.* I remember
the cook we rescued from jail, the drunken accountant,
the priest who had failed and the shattered, young
woman who hid in a closet and wailed.

The old gardener I startled day-dreaming one day,
I saw he had nothing, just his dank basement bay,
his sad eyes looked up, afraid I might judge, or perhaps
he'd told God he accepted his fate, for I felt
I withdrew from one in a sanctified state.

Not long ago I had it within to frighten myself with
this sort of thing; for it needed only a glimpse of
what might've been, of a featureless future,
for looking back then, everything seemed
to hang by a whim on a string.

Yet all that remains of such days is an odd love for
the broken; still, I wager that in some alternate
universe no different from this, our basement cot
waits as we work off what's owing, hang up our tools,
humbled, in pain, everything wasted, nothing was gained.

The Road from Toronto to Ottawa

You begin at your front stoop, then drive
four hours and thirty minutes, add an
an hour for coffee breaks and gas, and
maybe lunch. If you are in a rush you
may prefer the 401 and 416, in which
case I recommend Denny's at the Flying
J for its sandwich and its soup. But we are
not ones to hurry and to be honest have
never liked the stolid flatness of the easy
route nor the sprawling, green-hued
farmland that rarely seems to end.

My wife and I prefer the plodding way of
county roads, of rivers and bracken and
blueberry booths, the outcroppings
of ripple-coloured ancient rock and
eternal stands of pine and poplar.
We're drawn by village names like Tweed
and Kaladar, Silver Lake and Sharbot
Lake. I fancied as a boy the 'a' and
"o" were really 'e's and Sharbot Lake
a bowl that over-flowed with lime and
orange sherbet, the coolest thing on earth.

I have been following this path forever,
visiting uncles, cousins and friends, faith-
fully appearing at weddings and funerals
and once when I was still a youth to see
a girl who wasn't there. We worked here for

a year and married here. For decades it
was business brought me back, odd
requests that paid their way, more
fun then work, then foolish schemes
promising to make us rich but never did,
and now it is my daughter and her family.

It is strange to love something so plain and
undistinguished as a curving, backwoods
road, which is nothing when you think of
it but blacktop and some slaps of
paint. Yet I do love this rolling
passage that carries us forward to
the ones we love and inward into
memory. Listen how the asphalt
whirrs beneath the wheels and the
wind acknowledges nothing human
as it swooshes past the open window.
Such journeys are the best, the ones
that have no end.

Seafarers

In timelessness, destiny decrees us
seafaring peoples, born sovereign
over tides and tumbling sleep-ward

on breezes pungent with saltwater
and sea fauna, dreaming on winds
that forever carry Sinbad to his isle of

Auks and Odysseus home to Ithaca. Our
celestial maps and sextant are secure
at our sides, the bosun whistles and the

main sheet snaps and groans, sails hoisted
and wind-billowed and the black-billed
gulls cry each to each. Soon, night will

unfurl vast and spirit-haunted skies and
stars summon seafarers to wander the
dark-lit waters, whispering, unknown.

Darkness Visible

I am disarmed by such awesome humbling,
standing quietly on Africa's craggy cape,
gazing west toward fearsome Atlantic and
east to the warm salt waters of India, and
more strangely still, south beyond the murky,
slanting light that shades toward gradients of
shuttering darkness and on to that frigid
and alien face that at moments unbearable
and bleak God begins to show us.

My Cynical Friend the Sex Tourist

A friend since childhood has written
to expound on how strangely our paths
intertwine through time, even to the last
of days it seems, so it's hardly fitting

that I've become so distant. We grew
to men within a ball's toss of the other,
proceeded in parallel like brothers
through school, brewing hullabaloo

and nonsense as boys do, sometimes
playing the scholar, sometime the fool.
I married, grew stolid; we thought it cool
how he tossed aside rules and all was fine.

Friends admire that he chose the road
less travelled, but mourn where it led,
or how gross appetites that so long fed
on others might turn a man to craven toad.

I imagine myself tolerant, preferring
to pass no judgements. I will always
shake a hand, enjoy a laugh, nothing fazes
or startles me now, not even the erring

ways of one who once was close. We share
odds and ends like tokens in a cardboard
box – memories of early escapades, a hoard
of disassorted friends from varied lives, rare

that a friendship out-lasting wars and hatreds
and rollicking times long past might not fare
between his world gone cold and those I love
grown sacred.

Sailing on the Danforth

The west is an ember-billowed glow
where silver towers dream their dreams
but here the mist is rolling in
and corsairs from the evening shores
sail sky-blue boats by Greek cafes
while drowned men wait by alleyways.
And I'm full sail and gliding free
a sailor racing home from sea
full sail and swaggering down the street
the raw salt breeze in my face.

[Danforth Avenue is a road in Toronto which passes the city's
historic Greektown.]

The Smile

Lady of the velvet cape
blue as evening's azure skies
lady with dark chestnut eyes
shivved my heart
in spring-raw March
with a smile sudden
as a wheel of larks.

Phantom with the stole-
black hair,
my lady of a mislaid time,
why ever did you disappear
and leave behind
your smile?

What Lies Between

**The real constitution of things
Is accustomed to hide itself.**
- fragment attributed to Heraclitus

Divinity resides in forgetfulness
for what is missing does so by design
and illuminates the boundaries of the tactile.

What more could Heraclitus tell us?
Forgotten manuscripts reveal nothing,
but through their absence lend
transcendence to the simple text.

So it is with fragments.

In memory, a regret or suffering
like the symbol _n_ represents a series
too painful to contemplate in whole.

Or take for example Petronius
whose tales of debauchery survive
discontinuous as troubled recollections.
Wanderings   shipwrecks   lusts
islands severed from the main,
each odder still for what is
unexplained.

I wonder if it will be like this
In our separate howling hours.

When night spreads across abandoned
floors will we turn over the shards,
remembering the cool of a lover's spine or
the strange blue texture of December,
remembering an unspoiled summer's afternoon
and forgetting the barren stage, the relentless
hours that give such fragments their
luminous intensity?

The Way of All Guys

When I was a young man I knew everything
I strutted about and felt like a king.

My friends were no different I seem to recall
We shouldered the burden of knowing it all.

We soaked up our Sigmund and dabbled in Marx
And that was for starters, just for a lark.

The meaning of life and the coming of doom
Were questions we'd answer before it was noon.

And if it were night and we were drinking draft beer
A girlfriend would deconstruct Shakespeare's King Lear.

As for the whales in the ocean and the stars in the sky
They were quickly explained over coffee and rye.

But then as we stood at the top of our game
And here I hardly know who we should blame.

But life intervened like the slow stripping of gears
And all that we knew slipped into arrears.

I started a job, thinking they're in for a shock
When this clever new kid arrives on their block.

But things don't always go according to plan
When people don't realize: You is da Man.

A misunderstanding it seems had started to brew
That odd as it seems, I hadn't a clue.

And not just at work ~ this condition was spreading
As I discovered shortly after my wedding.

And then came the kids and threw me a loop
Even for diapers, I didn't know poop.

So maybe I wasn't as smart as I thought
Maybe I knew not a whole frigging lot.

But I would get tough, I would get mean
I'd quickly become a hard-charging machine

But it sure isn't easy, things don't come quick
When life turns around and gives you a kick.

But I kept at it and didn't surrender
I worked and thought till my brain grew quite tender.

I took in a lot as the years ticked away
But knew less and less, I'm sorry to say.

I learned nothing is certain, I'm sad to report
Not forever, the rainbow, or even the quark.

Not the music of Mozart, the moon or the law
Not even the insult that sticks in the craw.

Only wind over water and light on the beach
And everything, everything far beyond reach.

This wasn't a cop out, just the way the Path led
Through savannahs of hope and forests of dread.

So what do we know at the close of the day?
What ultimate wisdom can we finally relay?

What is the news, how do things fall?
Can we shout it in head lines 100 feet tall?

There is no knowing it seems in the end.
Not-knowing and dreams is all of it friend.

Not knowing and dreams and a beer we can share
The love of our women, our kids living near

The love for our families, our friends and our passions
And a good laugh at ourselves is always in fashion.

Poems For Younger Folk

I've Been to the Attic

I've been to the attic and guess what I saw,
some old photo albums and a dinosaur's jaw,
a trunk full of comics, a soldier's tin hat,
a stuffed alligator and somersault mat,
and oh, what I spied in a nook of the room —
coins that glimmered like Spanish doubloons!
Wherever I looked were marvels to view,
come with me now, I'll show them to you,
then on the roof, from our lonely crow's nest
we'll watch porpoises dancing far to the west.
It'll be so much fun, so much to explore
up to the attic and through the green door,
we'll play till the sun slips under the eaves,
till our moms call us home with evening's breeze.

Red-Winged Blackbird

I passed by a marsh on a gusty May day
and chanced on a blackbird swooping to play,
he trilled out a welcome, shot off in flight,
his black feathers shimmered in dancing sunlight,
his wing-tops were fired in orange-red hues,
above flashing gold glints and glimmering blues;
swerving and soaring, he rose skyward to sing,
remember this moment and forever love spring.

I wish ...

I wish I were bigger, a hundred feet tall
and strong as ten-thousand tigers in all;
with giant boots hoisted up to my knees,
away I would stride, stepping over the seas.

I wish I could run like the wind in a gale
or leap like a horse over valley and dale,
or better still wish I could fly like a dove,
for then I could visit the people I love.

But I'm really not big, so strong or that fast,
If I flew with the birds, I know I'd come last,
for I'm only six, and if you could just wait
in another two years, I'm going to be eight.

My Happy Birdfeeder

Sparrows and finches the summer long
flock to my feeder in hearty song,
Cardinals, blackbirds, blue jays too
fly close and chirp at the hullabaloo.

What a happy thing it is for me
to watch my friends on the balcony,
dart and swerve, then nibble seed,
sing with joy: "Here's all we need."

They think me such a silly dunce,
I'm always snookered out of lunch.
They dine like kings, then upwards soar,
and laugh as I pour seed once more.

Visit to the Mall

Pull on your gummy boots
and fasten up your jacket,
grab the mitts and woolen scarf
beside the sewing basket,
Mom is driving to the mall today,
the school day is through,
we'll ride the rolling-rocking horse
and see the petting zoo.

How I love those little creatures
with their soft and tender ways,
last year I pet a tiny sheep,
he answered with a "bey".
There were goats and deer
and donkeys, even ponies too,
the giant tortoise winked at me
and lamas nuzzled you.

That was one whole year ago,
but they're hoping that we'll call,
for I whispered loud our names to
each, saying we'd come back this fall.

The Stars in Summer

Late at night when
the owl who-o-s
and field mice scupper
through thatch and gutter,
then comes the blackest-
blues of night-time sky,
and stars like crystals
tossed up high
from giant hands
to startle souls
who strive and love
so far below.

It's then I long to lie
upon the grass
and sky-ward gaze,
and wonder at the
unexpected ways
that beauty sweeps
our hearts asway,
for marvel how the
old sparks-thrower sets
alight the vaulting
summer sky
to awe such simple folk
as you and I.

Leaping Love

We'll dance around the kitchen
we'll waltz off to Kowloon
we'll rhumba past the rainbow
and tap dance to the moon

We'll click our heels at midnight
and jump up to the stars
we'll samba toward the sunrise
and boogaloo to Mars

And when there's no more dancing
when our rocking days are through,
my heart will be hip-hopping
with its leaping love for you.

Geese in the Night

I gaze as you soar through star-vaulted night
with wings so gracefully moving in flight.
What vision compels and holds you to course,
what transcendent longings and mysterious force?
Creatures indifferent to man and his days,
who sings you the songs that dream you away?

Posted During Covid 19

Many zoo animals love
the quiet, others grow lonely
for our company

A Path in the Woods

The morning's so lovely, let's stroll down the way
where the farmer has piled his last bale of hay,
there's an ancient green forest of cedar and pine
rising west to the hills past the old village line.

For a trail that I love and calls in my dreams
starts by the road and heads off to a stream,
a walk of an hour, a jaunt for fine weather,
then it winds out of view and leads on to forever.

It's strewn with soft needles from trees up above,
and one day I'll wander this path that I love,
but won't you come with me? We'll walk side by each
past canyons and caverns, by fjords dark and deep.

Autumn in the City

We long to walk on autumn days
through parks and city alleyways,
to ponder beauty spinning out its dreams
of sun-flamed reds and golds and greens.

And to be alone, perhaps, to muse
upon the path that led us here today,
to this hilltop view or small café,
and on visions glimpsed from far away.

www.ingramcontent.com/pod-product-compliance
Lightning Source LLC
Chambersburg PA
CBHW031416160726
47993CB00003B/1258